Is forgiveness really free?

And other questions about grace,
the law and being saved

Michael Jensen

Is forgiveness really free?
And other questions about grace, the law and being saved
Part of the *Questions Christians Ask* series
© Michael Jensen/The Good Book Company, 2014
Reprinted 2014

Published by
The Good Book Company
Tel (UK): 0333 123 0880;
Tel (North America): (1) 866 244 2165
International: +44 (0) 208 942 0880
Email (UK): info@thegoodbook.co.uk
Email (North America): info@thegoodbook.com

Websites
UK & Europe: www.thegoodbook.co.uk
North America: www.thegoodbook.com
Australia: www.thegoodbook.com.au
New Zealand: www.thegoodbook.co.nz

ISBN: 9781909559783

Printed in the UK by CPI Group (UK) Ltd, Croydon, CR0 4YY
Design by André Parker

Contents

Introduction

Juliette had grown up in church, and never doubted the existence of God. She'd thought about the resurrection of Jesus from the dead and decided that she believed it.

But something was just not right.

She couldn't shake the feelings of guilt she had from her years of living with her boyfriend. He wasn't a Christian, and for a long time Juliette had stopped going to church altogether. Even though that was long in the past, nothing could shake the nagging sense that there was something that God still had against her—despite the fact that she had gone to him in prayer many times to seek forgiveness.

Matt, on the other hand, had never wavered from his faith. He was a well-read Christian, and had even considered studying at Bible college. However, he confessed to me, his pastor: "My heart is cold towards God". He explained that while he knew the *facts* of the gospel, he could feel no affection for God. Nothing made him feel really *alive* to Jesus.

Perhaps you can relate to one of these experiences, or even both. The funny thing is that for both Matt and Juliette the answer is the same.

They need to understand grace.

Grace is amazing

The most famous hymn ever written is about this special idea—grace. John Newton, the former slave trader, called it *Amazing Grace*. And what makes it amazing?

The key line of the hymn is the most shocking one:

that saved a wretch like me

A wretch?

In the 21st century, we are brought up to have better self-esteem than that. To call yourself "a wretch" means that you don't think you deserve anything at all. That you are helpless.

And yet, if we don't see this, we won't be able to see what grace is, and what it achieves. Grace is simply defined as "undeserved favour". It can't be earned: it must be given.

That's a description of what God has done for human beings in creating a beautiful and good world, filled with pleasure and delight. We didn't do a single thing to purchase the world we live in, or to make it. And yet we are here to enjoy it every day.

And "grace" describes what God did in sending his Son, the man Jesus Christ, to live among us as one of us, and to die for us on a bloody cross.

In 2 Corinthians 8 v 9, the apostle Paul writes:

> For you know the grace of our Lord Jesus Christ, that though he was rich, yet for your sake he became poor, so that you through his poverty might become rich.

That's a good explanation of what grace is. Jesus, as the Son of God, rich with all the unimaginable wealth of heaven, embraces the poverty of human life so that we have a share in the riches he left behind.

The purpose of this book

My aim in writing this book is to help you plunge into a deeper and richer experience of God's grace, so that it may make a huge difference in your life. It might be that you have never understood grace before. But it might be that you have forgotten what it means, too.

Matt didn't really understand the depths of his wretchedness before God—so he couldn't begin to grasp grace. Juliette had feelings of wretchedness, but refused to believe that God's acceptance of her was complete in Jesus.

Both of them needed to know God's grace not simply as an idea or concept—but personally, emotionally, and at the core of their being. They needed to know God's grace as you might know of a parent's love. It's the difference between knowing something is true, and knowing something is true for you.

Chapter 1

A precious word

As a former English teacher, I am known for being a bit particular about words. It irritates me when people are sloppy about them, or when people persistently misuse, or even abuse, a particular word. And I feel humiliated when someone discovers that I have been similarly inattentive to the way that words should work. I can never remember when to use "effect" and when to use "affect", for example.

To some people this might seem like fussiness—and, worse than that, fussiness over something that doesn't matter very much in the long run.

But I am firmly committed to my fussiness. I think words are worth being fussy over, because they are the tools of our communication, and because, when we miscommunicate with one another, we hurt each other.

There are some words which are so precious that

they become battlegrounds. If we do not agree on what "love" means, or "peace", then we will not be able to love or to have peace.

Of course, the difficulty in grasping the true meaning of words increases when we are dealing with words as they move between languages. Again, "love" is a famous example: the various Greek words we have classically translated as "love" are not the same as one another. Yet when we use the English word "love", we may be talking about erotic love or friendship or the delight in a particular flavour of ice cream. "I love Jenny" and "I love rum'n'raisin" do not mean the same thing at all.

"Grace" is one of these words. When we use it in English, we usually think of two things. First, some of us may think of that prayer which some people say before meals: "Let's say Grace".

Secondly, we think (well, I do) of Audrey Hepburn, that great actress of the silver screen, as the embodiment of this word. Why? Because she had a kind of virtuous elegance about her. She was great as only a twentieth-century film star could be great—far off, not a mere mortal, a real "star"—but she did not appear to be an arrogant or haughty person. She was "graceful" in her movements and in her manners; she was known not just for her on-screen achievements, but also for her charity work.

Is that what "grace" really is? There's something right about this use of the word to describe a person who is extremely regal and yet, without compromising their highness, is able to speak to mere mortals. The superior deigning to bless the inferior in some way is very close to the heart of what grace is.

Learning grace from what grace does

But theologically and biblically speaking, we need to start not with grace as it is exhibited by human beings, but grace as it comes from God himself. And in the great narrative of the Bible, the words we usually translate as "grace" (*hen* in Hebrew, and *charis* in Greek) generally refer to the way in which God approaches human beings to relate to them.

God's relationship with Israel is, of course, the prime example of this. God called them out of Egypt, where they were only slaves with no rights under an oppressive king, making bricks in the hot sun. And yet, without them in any way deserving it, God made them into a nation as his chosen people, his "treasured possession". He saved them from disaster through the Red Sea, and brought them into the land he had promised would be theirs.

And in so doing, he revealed his very own nature to them. One of the great moments of the story was at Mount Sinai, in the desert. There he said to Moses these words:

> The LORD, the LORD, the compassionate and gracious God, slow to anger, abounding in love and faithfulness, maintaining love to thousands, and forgiving wickedness, rebellion and sin. Yet he does not leave the guilty unpunished; he punishes the children and their children for the sin of the parents to the third and fourth generation.
>
> *Exodus 34 v 6-7*

11

It's worth reflecting on these words carefully, not least because they come at such an important point in the story of the Exodus, but also because they are words that come up more than once in the Old Testament. For instance, Jonah, dismayed that God is not going to punish Nineveh after all, *complains to the Lord about his own character* (Jonah 4 v 2)! These words have become a bit of a slogan summing up God's character, and rightly so.

These words also tell us what God's grace is by *showing us what God's grace does*. And what is that exactly? God shows his grace in *maintaining* his love even to those who do not deserve it by any stretch. And so, maintaining his love and being slow to anger requires from him forgiveness. His grace flows out in the forgiveness of "wickedness, rebellion and sin".

Make no mistake: there was plenty of that stuff in ancient Israel's history. One of the remarkable things about the Old Testament is the way in which it is such a "warts and all" account of the people it describes. This "Bible of Israel" continually reminds its readers that they are nothing without the grace and favour of the LORD.

But notice how Exodus 34 v 7 goes on to tell us that the LORD is not simply a pushover. Grace does not mean that sin and evil do not matter to God. Neither does grace mean that his justice is undermined. He does not, God says of himself, overlook the guilty or let them go unpunished.

This seems to be a contradiction at the heart of God's declaration about himself. How can he be both gracious and slow to anger, and yet proclaim himself the uncompromising punisher of sin? We can see this worked out in Israel's history as God repeatedly punishes their rebellion and evil-doing—though in doing so he aims at winning them back into the safe haven of his grace.

But this contradiction is only completely resolved at the cross of the Son of God, Jesus Christ. This is what the apostle Paul explains in his letter to the Romans, which has rightly been dubbed the "letter of grace". Paul asks this question about God's justice and mercy: *How can God be both just and righteous and justify the ungodly?* Paul's answer is that God has expressed his grace in the death of his Son, who himself suffered God's wrath against sin and opened up the way for Jews and Gentiles together to know peace with God.

> For all have sinned and fall short of the glory of God, and all are justified freely by his grace through the redemption that came by Christ Jesus.
>
> *Romans 3 v 23-24*

That is, God's favour is made available to human beings, definitively and beautifully, through the death of Jesus on the cross for sin.

That is grace in a nutshell. It's the love God shows to human beings when by rights there is nothing good they have earned from him. As Paul keeps saying: *You can't boast about grace, because it is given entirely as a gift.*

The story of grace, continued
But that's not the end of the story of grace. Paul some-

times makes it sound as if grace is like a thing that is *continually* given to us—talking about "God's abundant provision of grace", for example, in Romans 5 v 17.

Paul and the other New Testament writers were always concerned to maintain this understanding of the gospel of grace, because the instincts of our old sinful nature want to sneak self-achievement back into our lives. In a few centuries after the New Testament, much of the church had strayed from this understanding of grace to something quite different. Instead of something God shows to us in his love and mercy, "grace" became a thing that God gives in recognition of our virtue—for which he rewards us with our salvation.

It became commonplace in church teaching to suggest that we can receive this grace in particular through taking the sacraments—baptism and the Lord's Supper. Once we have received grace, we then go on to do good works by co-operating with this grace in us, and so earn the rewards that we deserve from God's hand.

The Reformers of the sixteenth century—Bible-believing Christians like John Calvin and Martin Luther—would have none of this. They argued that "grace" as it was being taught was nothing like grace in the Bible. They understood that salvation is by grace alone, or (to use the Latin slogan) *sola gratia*. There is no combination of grace and works involved in the rescue of human beings. There can't be, since sin is actually so bad that human beings will never co-operate in their salvation.

The Reformers rediscovered from the Bible that true grace is entirely a matter of God's favour towards us, made possible by Jesus Christ's death on the cross. We are not accepted by God because of the good works that grace produces; we are accepted because of his grace in order to *do* the good works that it produces. The things we do cannot ever be the reason for our salvation, as Paul explains in Romans 11 v 6, because...

... if it were, grace would no longer be grace.

Grace no longer grace? That's right: if there's a suggestion that grace is merely God's *help* for us when we plead for his favour, then it is no longer really grace. He has not shown us his grace at all. It would be like giving us a Ferrari but not giving us the keys.

That's why, properly understood, the word "grace" is so precious—because it contains the reason why the Christian message really is good news. God's grace to us in Christ is not conditional on our performance in any way, or upon our taking part in certain rituals, or on our having confessed in precise detail everything we can think of we have done wrong. Those false views of grace only lead to a life filled with guilt, uncertainty and a lack of assurance. Those who think of grace like that will walk through this world fearful that God is displeased with them.

But if you have understood that the grace you have received from God is free and complete, then you have a different experience. You can walk through life confident that God is smiling upon you now, and will not condemn you at the end—because of his grace towards you through Christ.

What is "common grace"?

There is only one God, and he has the same character whatever he does. If he saves by grace, then surely he must also create by grace as well.

Our experience of the grace of the gospel of Jesus Christ enables us to see the world around us as an expression of that same character of God. Life itself with all its pleasures and its delights is not the product of some remorseless process with no guiding principle except efficiency. Far from it: it is the product of our generous God, who grants to all creatures life without them earning a single breath of it (Acts 17 v 25).

And even those who don't recognise God enjoy it. They inhabit a good and beautiful world, and enjoy it, because of the generosity of the Creator—who didn't need to make the world, but did so because of his gracious character. We enjoy not just the beauty and bounty of creation, but also the warmth of human families, art, music and creativity, and above all love, which always has its origins in God (see 1 John 4 v 7).

This is what theologians call "common grace", as opposed to "special grace", which is what God shows towards those who trust in Christ. Although we all enjoy common grace, it does not save us. In fact the Bible teaches that when we receive God's good gifts, but fail to acknowledge him or give thanks to him for them, we confirm our own guilt before him (Romans 1 v 20-21).

Paul suggests in Acts 17 v 27 that one of the reasons God shows *common* grace to us is so that it might lead us to seek God and discover his *special* grace in Christ.

Chapter 2

Is forgiveness really free?

The thing that people find hardest to believe about the gospel of Jesus Christ, by far, is not that it involves a man rising from the dead; it is not that it involves believing in a personal deity who made the world with a word; it is not even that a good God could allow a world where there is suffering.

Far more difficult to believe is that God's grace is really free.

We have such a deeply ingrained doubt about grace that we have trouble hearing and understanding the message about God's free gift. We are so used to living in the world of what we might call "ungrace" that we cannot bring ourselves to really understand what the world of grace might actually look like. We hear the gospel of ungrace every day in sayings like:

■ *There is no such thing as a free lunch.*

- *Money doesn't grow on trees.*
- *The world doesn't owe you a living.*
- *There is no gain without pain.*

These are the principles of the world of ungrace. It's a world where you get what you deserve. It's a world in which you look with pride on your achievements and hide your failures in shame. It's a world in which you are constantly judged, marked, critiqued, fed back to and evaluated. It's a world in which you take any advantage you can, because only the fittest, or smartest, or prettiest survive.

The idea of *karma*, where (to quote the Australian pop group Savage Garden) "what you get is what you give returned", just seems so much more logical and fair.

Although I know about grace, and I have even experienced grace, the old mental habit of ungrace is stubbornly persistent.

I work to bolster my list of achievements because it makes me feel like someone of whom I can be proud.

I judge others for their failures, and carry my grievances with me like a handbag. I am not just the eldest son in my family; I am also the eldest son in Jesus' famous story (Luke 15 v 11-32) .

When it comes to our standing before God, we fall into one of two errors of ungrace. We either presume on God's favour, subconsciously believing that God's free gift to us in Christ comes to us actually because we are really rather loveable and deserving; or we think that we could *never* be acceptable to God because we are really rather unacceptable to everyone else.

Strangely, sometimes the same person can hold to these two thoughts at the same time.

Jesus' crazy economics

This idea of God's grace is the beating heart of Jesus' teaching. He never mentions the actual word "grace", but he teaches about it constantly. There's the parable of the lost son welcomed home by the father, despite everything (Luke 15 v 11-32). There's the one about the banquet which is thrown open to those who by rights can't expect an invitation (Matt 22 v 1-14).

But the parable which causes us the greatest degree of bewilderment is, I think, the parable of the workers in the vineyard.

Jesus said to them …

"For the kingdom of heaven is like a landowner who went out early in the morning to hire workers for his vineyard. He agreed to pay them a denarius for the day and sent them into his vineyard.

"About nine in the morning he went out and saw others standing in the market-place doing nothing. He told them, 'You also go and work in my vineyard, and I will pay you whatever is right.' So they went.

"He went out again about noon and about three in the afternoon and did the same thing. About five in the afternoon he went out and found still others standing around. He asked them, 'Why have you been standing here all day long doing nothing?'

"'Because no one has hired us,' they answered.

"He said to them, 'You also go and work in my vineyard.'

"When evening came, the owner of the vineyard said to his foreman, 'Call the workers and pay them their wages, beginning with the last ones hired and going on to the first.'

"The workers who were hired about five in the afternoon came and each received a denarius. So when those came who were hired first, they expected to receive more. But each one of them also received a denarius. When they received it, they began to grumble against the landowner. 'These who were hired last worked only one hour,' they said, 'and you have made them equal to us who have borne the burden of the work and the heat of the day.'

"But he answered one of them, 'I am not being unfair to you, friend. Didn't you agree to work for a denarius? Take your pay and go. I want to give the one who was hired last the same as I gave you. Don't I have the right to do what I want with my own money? Or are you envious because I am generous?'

"So the last will be first, and the first will be last."

Matthew 19 v 28 – 20 v 16

The outline of the story is simple. The owner of the vineyard has some work he needs doing. So, first thing in the morning, he finds some workers and agrees with them a full day's wage. But the work isn't getting done, and he decides that he will hire some other fellows to help out. So he goes back to the market-place where the as-yet unhired workers are standing around, and he calls them in, telling them somewhat vaguely that he will pay them "whatever is right".

He does this at 9am, at noon, at 3pm; and then, with the shadows of the day lengthening, at 5pm. That's five different groups of workers, some of whom have worked a grueling twelve-hour day by the time it is all finished.

Then, when it's time to settle up the payroll, the land-owner hands out *exactly the same pay* to each worker.

It's a disastrous piece of workplace relations, isn't it? You can imagine how the first group of workers feel when they see what is going on. It is massively, blatantly and completely unfair. They have worked the whole sweaty day. The last group only chipped in at the end for an hour. And yet... the same reward is given to all. No wonder someone speaks up and says: "These who were hired last worked only one hour ... and you have made them equal to us who have borne the burden of the work and the heat of the day".

I hope you can see his point and feel something of his pain.

We all have an acute sense of fairness. It was taught to us in pre-school and probably even before, and it lasts our whole lives. We don't like unfairness, especially when it is directed against us.

I saw an experiment on YouTube, where two caged capuchin monkeys were rewarded for giving the scientist a stone. The first monkey was given a grape for each stone. The second monkey was given a piece of cucumber. The monkey who was given the cucumber was at first quite happy with his reward. But when he saw that the other monkey was being given sweet, luscious grapes, he started to become angry, and he threw the cucumber back at the scientist. Who wants cucumber when a grape is on offer?

This video was used in a talk by a biologist[1] as evidence of moral behaviour in animals. And it was, after a fashion. Though perhaps it better illustrated the reverse: that what we call "moral" behaviour is really no such thing, but just what monkeys would do in the same situation.

Let's be frank; Jesus' vineyard owner has been quite unfair. And I'll bet it made employing workers the next day a bit more difficult, too.

But he defends himself by saying:

I am not being unfair to you, friend. Didn't you agree to work for a denarius? Take your pay and go. I want to give the one who was hired last the same as I gave you. Didn't I have the right to do what I want with my own money? Or are you envious because I am generous?

He has a point: he has not been dishonest and he has

---

1   http://goo.gl/WvT1cS, accessed 11/2013.

not dishonoured any contracts or agreements. The workers knew what they were getting when they started, and worked happily for that. It was only when they saw what others were getting that it became an issue for them. What are the grounds for their complaint, really? After all, no injustice has been done, no promise has been broken.

But it still feels uncomfortable. Especially when Jesus says that this is what the kingdom of heaven is like— where the last will be first, and the first will be last. We don't like things being so out of kilter, or so unexpected. We are used to the economy of exchange: where equal work gets equally paid; where debts accumulate, and interest is earned, and taxes are inevitable; where everything has a price.

But here, in the kingdom of heaven, the human way of ordering things is overturned. We are dealing with an economy of grace. And what does that look like? How does that operate?

The way the kingdom works

The kingdom of heaven contains people I wouldn't choose, that's for sure. It contains people who haven't served all their lives as decent, honourable citizens. It contains people who have committed all manner of crimes. It admits people despite everything and not because of anything.

It operates that way because of whose kingdom it is. It belongs to the Father of our Lord Jesus Christ, who in the beginning made the world not from necessity but out of the wealth of his freedom, and out of the pure generosity of his character.

God's economy is the economy not of the wage, but of the gift. Not, I hasten to add, the sort of manipulative gifts we give—the bottle of wine to the client, the gift given to one who loves us, or whose love we want to purchase. The giving of the divine gift springs entirely from his freedom to give.

And the pattern of his giving is extraordinary: he gives not because he is impressed, but because he can. He gives to those who least deserve it because it shows us that what comes from God is not a wage that we have earned, but a gift out of the overflow of his heart.

He doesn't *have* to give: he *wants* to.

I once went into a prison to visit a friend of mine who works as a chaplain there. To be honest, I was going to see if the gospel of God's grace was true. Could it really work for people on the inside? Let's not be romantic about it: people are locked away because they have done some pretty bad stuff. We generally don't put people in prison just for speeding or dropping litter. By any measure, prisoners are rightly unacceptable people.

The answer to my question came in the form of a violent offenders' Bible study which I attended. I sat and listened to a young man who had been in prison long enough already that I knew he had done something truly hideous. *Was it murder?* Could have been. I was afraid to ask.

And yet there he was—praying with me, reading the Bible with me, a brother in Christ.

It's an outrage, really. That kind of person is not the

sort you'd want to have in your church. They don't deserve to be there.

But the God of Jesus Christ is the God of such outrages. And here's the question that Jesus' parable is asking us: can we live with these divine outrages? Can we live with a God who doesn't recognise the pecking order that we're committed to? Can we live with a God who reverses the normal order of things? Because if you can't, I'm sorry, but you don't have an alternative.

This is why the parables of Jesus don't address us as those who are outsiders, but as those who think we are insiders. They force us to remember who we are: we are the children of God's grace. And as a result we have no basis for pride.

But we do have plenty of grounds for joy...

Grace and me

My own awakening to free forgiveness—to God's grace—came when I was about 16 years old.

I am, as I said, the eldest son. And I was the eldest son of a ministry family. I went to church and Sunday school, and never really rebelled. I knew all the answers, and it was kind of nice being a bit of a specialist in at least one subject on the school timetable (I went to a church school).

I was not much of a rebel, at least not publicly or openly. Mainly, I wanted to keep the appearance of being onside with the whole Christian thing, and I wasn't courageous enough to be defiant.

In retrospect, I was habitual in two sins: *lying* and *pride*. I had the smug satisfaction of thinking I was born into the Christian faith and knew that the behaviour of my classmates was reprehensible. The view from the moral high-ground was spectacular. *Thank God* (I imagine my younger self praying) *that I am not like those other kids…*

But of course, I did enjoy my moments of doing what my parents did not want me to do. Only, I concealed them well with dishonesty.

Was I a Christian at the time? I think so. But I didn't understand: I thought grace was for people who were in the throes of becoming a Christian dramatically—the gang member, the drug addict, the prostitute, the slave trader. That was amazing grace; but that was not for me. I was a little Pharisee.

It took a couple of Christian friends in their early twenties to show me that the grace of God was for me as well. To show me, in fact, that there is no other option than grace.

They asked me: was I a sinner? Well, of course I was—that was the correct answer.

"You can't simply be born into Christian faith," they said. I had to agree, although I felt that I hadn't had much choice about whether to be a Christian or not.

"Well, it is time to decide," they said! "And the thing to know is this: that your sin is greater than you think; but that God forgives you, by the cross of Jesus Christ.

"Yes, he forgives you: not because you are impressive and likeable and a morally decent fellow, or because you are a member of a holy family, but because of his great love for you."

This to me was a life-changing realisation. You could

build a life on that knowledge. All the uncertainties of knowing who I was were completely swept away—not because I had found an identity, but because God had called me his son, in Jesus. And since he was the one who was doing it, I couldn't lose it. It was an amazing moment of security and assurance. It told me who I was and who I am.

It is still what gets me out of bed in the morning, 25 years later.

How do I get grace?

You can only receive grace by faith. Otherwise, it is not grace: it can't have the nature of a gift if it is earned.

But what is faith? In English we use the word in a number of overlapping ways. Sometimes it simply means a religion, as in "the Christian faith" or "the Islamic faith". Sometimes we think of "having faith" as "believing some things to be true and other things not to be true".

But in the context of receiving grace, the Bible talks of faith as something like "giving yourself in personal trust to the God who promises". When God made his promises to Abraham, Abraham believed him—in other words, he had faith that God would honour his promises. And that shaped Abraham's life from then on.

So when Paul writes in Ephesians 2 v 8: *"For it is by grace that you have been saved, through faith"*, he is speaking about how the Ephesian believers took hold of grace by believing God's promises. That same way of receiving grace is available to you today. If you want to receive this great gift of forgiveness, just take it as a gift from God, who promises to forgive you through Christ. And let that shape your life from now on.

Chapter 3

If grace is free, is it worth anything?

What is the most valuable thing that you own?

At first it sounds like a relatively easy question, and it wouldn't be hard to think of the answer in terms of some simple possession or perhaps an investment. You may have filled in an insurance form that asks you to put a monetary value next to each of your possessions, just in case they are destroyed by fire, flood or tempest, or in case you get robbed; and so you actually know which is the most valuable item on your list. Is it your car or a precious ring you've been given or inherited?

But the idea that value can only be measured in monetary terms is very one-dimensional and neglects the personal and human dimension of our attachments. What we value most are the things that are beyond value; or the things that are not worth anything in and of themselves but which have a particular significance for us. They are better described as "precious".

Recently, my parents moved out of a large family home to a smaller residence. This meant trawling through all the strange things that they had kept over the years, like my stamp collection and my primary-school assignments. Now, these things have no monetary value at all. But they were of value to me. In fact, for me, some of these things were irreplaceable and incredibly precious. No doubt my descendants will throw them out in time.

More than that, when I think of preciousness I think not of the things I like, but the people I love: my wife, my children. When someone in grief says: "I would give anything to have back the one I have lost", it is not too hard to understand what they are saying. When a court tries to compensate a person for, say, the loss of their spouse in an accident, we get something of the absurdity of even trying to put a price on the loss.

The precious pearl

In his parable of the pearl, Jesus wants us to think very deeply about what is precious to us.

> Again, the kingdom of heaven is like a merchant looking for fine pearls. When he found one of great value, he went away and sold everything he had and bought it. *Matthew 13 v 45-46*

Imagine a merchant. His business is perhaps the sale of

fine jewels and luxury goods. And he's in search of fine pearls. Why? Because he is a merchant. He's a business-man, looking to make a profit. Perhaps we should think of him travelling in search of his goods as far as the Red Sea—a location where we know pearls were found in the first century.

And make no mistake, pearls were the most precious jewel of the ancient world. This, at least, was the opinion of the Roman author Pliny, writing in the first century. His contemporary, the historian Suetonius, wrote that the Roman general Vitellius, emperor for eight months in 69 AD, financed an entire military campaign by sell-ing just one of his mother's pearl earrings. Cleopatra is said to have dissolved one of her pearl earrings in a glass of wine and drunk it, just so she could win a bet with Mark Anthony that she could consume the wealth of an entire country in a single meal. Recounting the story (and no doubt exaggerating a bit—who doesn't?), Pliny estimated the value of Cleopatra's pair of pearls at 10 million sesterces. It is impossible to say exactly what that means in today's money, but the fact that an or-dinary soldier would have earned 1000 sesterces a year puts it in perspective. It is a phenomenal sum.

So this merchant is after the kind of goods that might make him a very tidy profit, if he plays it right. That's his business.

But then he makes a surprising discovery: *a single pearl of immense value.* And, on finding this one pearl of very great value, he does something rather odd: he goes out and sells everything he has to buy it.

It's a slightly strange moment, because we are led to

think of him as a businessman, and it is unusual for a wise businessman to confine his portfolio to a single investment. It is an inherently risky strategy from a commercial point of view, because he has concentrated his entire wealth in this one object. He has made no back-up plan. It is not as though he has found a bargain, either: Jesus doesn't tell the story as if the merchant has found the pearl at the back of some antique shop somewhere in Alexandria, going for a few pieces of silver. This pearl is of great price, and it costs the merchant everything he has.

You can imagine him returning to his family after his business trip and trying to explain to his wife why the family home and its contents are up for sale.

What has enticed him?

It is the pearl.

This single fine pearl has hooked him. There's something almost obsessive about his behaviour—as if he has not simply found a way to make a fortune, but has fallen in love with the jewel. It has become the thing that he simply must possess, even if it destroys him as a businessman and makes his family life extremely difficult.

His behaviour suggests that the pearl is not simply a white lump, but a gem of extraordinary fascination and beauty. That's the interesting thing about precious jewels; they are valuable because of their rarity and beauty. They have no particular function that makes them valuable, at least not primarily. They do not gain their worth because we can put them to use in the service of some industry; they do not help us to feed a city, or guarantee our health, or protect us from enemies. They don't do anything.

They just are. They are simply compelling for their own sake. Their value lies in the awe that they create. And in this case, the single great pearl is so compelling that it causes this merchant to behave like a drug addict—with such singular focus that it makes ordinary life almost completely impossible. Desire for the pearl has completely taken him over.

He reminds me of the creature Gollum from *The Lord of the Rings*. The merchant's pearl is his "precious". We would think of him as unbalanced—a man who has lost interest in everything except this one beautiful thing. But the point of Jesus' story is to commend the man as wise. The person who does *not* treat the Kingdom of God like this is the one who has lost his mind. Why? Because the pearl is worth it. Because the kingdom of heaven is worth it.

Free, but not cheap

Now, that should make us think carefully. Notice in the first place that Jesus didn't say that the kingdom of heaven is like *the pearl* of great value, but that it is like *the merchant seeking* the pearl of great value, and his actions when he finds it. Jesus is directing our attention not simply to the pearl but to the response the pearl gets from the one who recognises its beauty.

It isn't the only reference to searching and seeking that we come across in Matthew's Gospel. In the Sermon on the Mount (Matthew 5 – 7) Jesus says:

> Seek first [God's] kingdom and his righteousness.
>
> *Matthew 6 v 33*

Indeed, a theme of the Sermon on the Mount is that God's rule of justice, peace and righteousness is something that you have to *long* for in order to find. It is given to those who look for it—those who hunger and thirst for righteousness, those who ask, seek and knock (see Matthew 5 v 6; 7 v 7-8). It is worth being obsessive about. If we only appreciated what God's kingdom was, we'd give up anything and everything to be a part of it. Our whole understanding of the value and significance of all other things would be transformed if only we knew how singularly precious the kingdom of heaven is.

But the complication of the parable for me is this:

> *God's grace comes for free,*
> *but it costs everything*
> *you have to get it.*

How can this be?

Well, we need to recognise the limits of the illustration. The merchant *buys* the pearl. It is expensive. A poor man would simply not have a chance in this story. It seems he would be priced out of the kingdom of heaven.

But that's not what Jesus is saying here. Rather, he is saying: *The grace of God is free, but it is not cheap.* We tend to think of those things that don't cost us anything as not really worth having at all—as somewhat disposable. I know of instances where people have put a ticket price on an event they were organising just to give the impression it was worth coming to—as a kind of mental trick.

But the kingdom of heaven is not disposable, or even recyclable. It is not made of plastic. It is, like the pearl, unique and beautiful. It is utterly compelling—and to such a degree that if you grasp it the right way, it will take over your life. Dietrich Bonhoeffer, the German pastor and theologian who was executed by the Nazis for his part in a plot to kill Hitler, said: "When Christ calls a man, he bids him come and die".

But this is not sad news, since the one who dies for the sake of Jesus and the gospel, the one who leaves behind all he has, the one who hates her mother and brother even—that person is blessed, according to Jesus. That person will have, in the kingdom of heaven, all that they have left behind, and much, much more besides (Matthew 19 v 29).

Selfish motives?

But then our instincts for ungrace kick in. We think: *Well then, isn't this actually selfish thinking? Isn't seeking the treasure of the kingdom of heaven simply a displaced form of greed? Isn't it just self-interest, the result of a sound calculation?*

But gaining the kingdom of heaven is not simply a transaction. Remember the disturbing obsessiveness of the merchant—that he loved the beautiful, singular pearl for its own sake, and not for its usefulness. It was not a means to some end for him. It was simply itself.

And so it is with the kingdom of heaven: to long for it, and to seek for it is *not to wish yourself rich*. It is to long for God himself; and to long to belong to the world where God's peace, and justice, and righteousness are established everywhere; and to long for the world finally to bear the fruit that even now is ripening.

The kingdom of heaven is beautiful; and the significance of its beauty is that to long for it is not to calculate your own selfish ends, but to desire with every fibre of your being to be part of its way of life. It is not to desire to own it, but to hunger to be owned *by it*—to be owned by the King of heaven himself.

The kingdom of heaven is valuable in just the way the people we love are precious to us. It is beyond economics. And it is like this because in it God shows us, not his accounting skills, but his own costly love. Love is what makes this treasure priceless. Since God, out of his great love, has given himself to us freely in his Son, then the only worthy response is to give him ourselves.

This parable challenges us to remember that here we have a magnificent obsession. If we "get" the kingdom of heaven, then we should not be surprised to find that what we value and how we count value are completely changed. We should be less surprised than we are at the baffled stares of our family and friends.

We should be happier to take risks with our worldly goods in light of our heavenly treasure. We should be less concerned about being socially acceptable and—worst of all—nice.

And we should never forget that the proper response

to the free grace of God is to follow Christ with everything we have.

It is striking to me that Jesus' parables of grace aren't simply about telling us that God freely forgives: they always point us to the fact that truly grasping free forgiveness means having an utterly altered life. We are not meant simply to be believers, but followers; or, better, being a believer *means* being a follower.

Why can't God just forgive?

The cross of Jesus is the heart of God's forgiveness of sins. It is the heartbeat of grace. But why can't God just forgive us, without the gruesome business of the cross?

We need to understand what forgiveness really involves. When you forgive someone, you aren't just shrugging your shoulders at them (that's not forgiveness; that's simply denial). Your forgiveness actually judges their actions as wrong. But you are also bearing the consequences for their actions on yourself, rather than seeking to exact vengeance or punishment from the person who has wronged you.

That's what happens between God and human beings. We sin, and deserve punishment. But on the cross, the Son of God took the punishment we deserve, and in doing so made it possible for God's wrath against sinners to be turned aside.

That means that God's forgiveness is *real* forgiveness. Not some kind of clever accounting trick. God doesn't tell us a lie—"never mind, your sin didn't matter that much; I love you anyway". We can see that sin is horrifically bad, and that God thinks it is deserving of judgement, by looking at the cross.

But we can also see that a genuine offer of personal forgiveness is on the table—because the painful penalty of our sin has been displayed to the world in the death of Jesus.

Chapter 4

Why does God give grace to some and not to others?

For he chose us in him before the creation of the world to be holy and blameless in his sight. In love he predestined us for adoption to sonship through Jesus Christ, in accordance with his pleasure and will—to the praise of his glorious grace, which he has freely given us in the One he loves.

Ephesians 1 v 4-6

God gives his grace to those who do not deserve it. That's what makes it what it is—grace. It removes human pride, because there's nothing in it that we can call our own except that which has been given to us. Even the decision for our salvation rests not with us, but with God.

A dark side to grace?

This sounds like good news, and so it is. But is there a

dark side to grace? Is God's decision to bestow his favour on some undeserving sinners and not on others simply evidence that he acts on a whim? Does he simply decide on the basis of some random principle—a divine throw of the dice perhaps? Is grace simply luck masquerading under another name?

In which case, is God less of a kind Father and more of a tyrant? Why, if he can give his grace to some, does he not give his grace to all?

We should recognise that it is a question with a personal dimension, too. Some people—people we love—don't respond to the gospel. Some did once, but sadly no longer do. What of them?

This is one of the most knotty problems in Christian theology, and it has led plenty of Christian theologians to propose a compromise on grace itself. The Bible clearly teaches that God chooses us "before the creation of the world", as it says at the start of this chapter.

How does he do that? If grace is not to seem arbitrary and unjust, then surely there must be some condition from the human side which triggers it. Perhaps there is something in us, be it ever so small, that God recognises as worthy of grace. Or perhaps he can see that we are trying as hard as we can. Or perhaps it is our membership of the institutional church that marks us out. Or perhaps (and this is quite an ingenious way of thinking about it) God looks down the length of human history and sees ahead of time who will respond to him, and so chooses those people.

The problem with all of these answers is that they make grace something other than what it is: the free gift of God. It becomes reliant on something that we offer him, however small.

What does the Bible actually say?

We are not the first to think about this. In fact—and I find this reassuring—the authors of the Bible wrestled with the very dilemma we are talking about, without giving us a cheap answer. In Romans chapters 9 – 11, Paul asks with some agony: *Why haven't many Israelite people responded to the gospel?*

In response, we can summarise the Bible's teaching in this way:

1. **God's offer of salvation is made to all people.** His love is for the world (John 3 v 16), and he does not want anyone to die in their sins.

2. **Nonetheless, not all people are to be saved.** There are those who stubbornly and tragically reject God's declaration of amnesty, and remain at war with him.

3. **It is God who chooses, or elects, those who belong to him.** As Jesus said: "All those the Father gives me will come to me, and whoever comes to me I will never drive away" (John 6 v 37).

4. **That means, inevitably, that God does not choose others.** Why? Paul's response to this question is to say: *Well, actually God has the absolute right as the creator of all things to do what he wishes with what he has made* (Romans 9 v 14-26). We have no appeal to a higher court; God the creator is not to be condemned from the human side simply because we do not understand his mind.

This seems like an acrid-tasting morsel to chew on. But we need to pause and hear what Paul is saying. He isn't saying *God creates some people merely so he can enjoy condemning them.* He is saying rather: *If God did act in this way, we'd have no cause for complaint against him.* The "if" is a crucial "if"; and it shows us what Paul is trying to do here. He is trying to draw our attention away from the question, because implicit in the question is the attempt to pass judgment on God.

We do not know the mind of God on this matter, and it does us no good to second guess him. The more we try to second guess God in the particulars of life, the more we get it wrong.

Grace that reassures us

This is crucial for us to see, because the doctrine of grace reminds us that those who have faith have it because of the work of God in them, pure and simple. We are not told who these people are in the final analysis. We cannot peer into the hearts of men and women and know what is really there. That will no doubt surprise us!

The point of the New Testament teaching about grace is not to make us anxious but precisely the opposite— which means that if it is causing concern, we've probably misunderstood it. We are meant to be reassured.

That's the point of the great first chapter of Ephesians: *Don't worry if your faith seems weak and uncertain, and if you are being persecuted. You were chosen in Christ from before the foundation of the world, and you stand secure in him. Your salvation does not rely on your uncertain moods, or on your confidence, or on your progress. It is built on an entirely solid foundation—on Jesus Christ.* And that in itself tells us where our gaze should be.

I do not know why or on what basis God chooses some and not others. Or rather, I can tell that he chooses the weak things of the world to shame the strong, as Paul explains in 1 Corinthians 1 v 27. But aside from that one strange condition—I have no idea.

Is God unjust?

Does God's unexplained choice of some and not others make him unjust? *No.* Not only does that accusation fail simply because God has the *right* to act as he sees fit, it also neglects the more important fact that this is the Father of Jesus Christ, who died on the cross for sin.

The extraordinary love of God poured out to us in the costly suffering of Jesus gives us every confidence that the God we are dealing with is not moody, arbitrary or capricious. He is the God who has shown time and time again in his dealings with his people that he is utterly faithful to his promises, and will go to extraordinary lengths to protect and care for his children. More than that, he is the sovereign Lord of all, and is shaping history to his purposes, so that he might accomplish all things "for the good of those who love him, who have been called according to his purpose" (Romans 8 v 28).

Is this answer simply a dodge, or a cop-out? Would it be better to have one of the compromise answers that I presented earlier? I think the answer is a definite "no" to both questions. We should assume that, since we are fallen and finite beings, full understanding of the ways of God will be beyond us. That doesn't mean we should stop seeking to understand God and what he does—not at all. But it does mean that, when we find a problem that we can't resolve simply, we shouldn't despair.

Can grace be taken away?

This is a question which worries many people for two reasons. First, we worry about family and friends who once were professing faith and have since walked away from the faith. Was their faith genuine? Will they one day return?

Secondly, we are worried because we know how weak we are. Could I commit some sin that might jeopardise my salvation? What about the great warning passages of the book of Hebrews, which seem to imply that we are hanging on to our salvation by the skin of our teeth? Am I "once saved, always saved"?

The best way to respond to this question is to focus not on ourselves but on the faithfulness of God. What is God like? He is faithful to his promises, and he has given us the Holy Spirit as the guarantee that we will receive everything he has promised his people (Ephesians 1 v 13-14). He has not spared his own Son, but has rescued us at great cost (Romans 8 v 32). We should then have confidence that he is committed to his own word. This is, in fact, the message of Hebrews: *"Let us then approach God's throne of grace with confidence, so that we may receive mercy and find grace to help us in our time of need"*. (Hebrews 4 v 16)

But the author also reminds, cajoles and warns his readers: *"So do not throw away your confidence; it will be richly rewarded. You need to persevere so that when you have done the will of God, you will receive what he has promised"* (Hebrews 10 v 35-36). Why would he need to do that, if their salvation was secure?

It is because these warnings and reminders are the very way in which God spurs us on to keep trusting Christ to be saved.

As a pastor, it is the person who is quite "laid back" about their salvation who I am most worried about—since they clearly do not really understand the value of what they have been given. The confidence that Hebrews speaks about is not a confidence that we are saved because of some past decision or prayer of commitment; but rather confidence in God, and that also means a right fear of him.

Can grace be taken away? The right answer is not "yes" or "no", but: *God is faithful: cling onto him with all your might.*

Chapter 5

What place does Old Testament law have in the life of grace?

Jesus: "Do not think that I have come to abolish the Law or the Prophets; I have not come to abolish them but to fulfil them. For truly I tell you, until heaven and earth disappear, not the smallest letter, not the least stroke of a pen, will by any means disappear from the Law until everything is accomplished." *Matthew 5 v 17-18*

Paul: "For sin shall no longer be your master, because you are not under the law, but under grace." *Romans 6 v 14*

The church building that I went to growing up was not ornately built. In fact, it was rather plain. This meant that the huge plaques pinned on the front wall stood out even more starkly. On them were written the Ten Commandments in a kind of medieval lettering (which made them look all the more fearsome).

The story of the delivery of the Ten Commandments

to Moses is even more dramatic than their appearance on the wall of my church building—which sadly burnt down several years ago. Moses comes down from Mount Sinai, from his encounter with the holy God, with his two tablets of stone, to an awestruck Israel. The first time he does this he smashes the tablets in rage because he sees the Israelites mucking around with the golden calf—breaking a central command of the law even as they receive it: "You shall have no other gods before me" (Exodus 20 v 3).

It's extraordinary stuff. The Ten Commandments were given to Israel—along with 603 others—not simply as a *suggestion* but as a rule for life in God's land under God's authority. This is what made Israel who they were. The Law was a distinctive moral and ceremonial pattern for their communal living, telling them what festivals to celebrate, who they could marry, what they could eat and what they should do when they had a period, or got spots.

When you read Psalm 119, which is a kind of love song to the *Torah* (the Hebrew name for the law), you get a picture of what the study and observance of the law might have meant to an Israelite mind. In Psalm 19 v 7 and 10, we hear these memorable words:

> The law of the Lord is perfect, refreshing the soul. The statutes of the Lord are trustworthy, making wise the simple … They are more precious than gold, than much pure gold; sweeter than honey, than honey from the honeycomb.

Pure gold and oozing honey: that's pretty powerful imagery, especially in a culture with no refined sugar!

The law now?

But what of Christians now? What role is the Old Testament law meant to have in the life of Christian believers? How and on what day should Christians observe the Sabbath, for example? What did it mean for Paul to say: "You are not under the law, but under grace" (Romans 6 v 14)? Did he mean by this that grace and the law are in opposition to one another? If so, in what way?

Had the sweet taste of the law become suddenly bitter?

There are indeed some pretty strong statements about the law in the New Testament, particularly from Paul, suggesting, in Romans 7 for example, that Christians are "slaves not under the old written code but in the new life of the Spirit." The law made us slaves. It could not save us. The regulations and rituals of the Old Testament were shadows of the things that were to come in Christ, and not by themselves able to save anyone. When Paul introduces the fruit of the Spirit in that extraordinary passage at the end of Galatians, he also says "against such things there is no law" (Galatians 5 v 23), as if to say: *law-thinking completely misses the point when it comes to the gospel of Christ.*

The question of the role of God's law in the Christian life has proved extremely controversial in the history of Christianity. Most Christian readers of the Old Testament will recognise that the Old Testament law is the word of God, and needs to be taken with all the seriousness that this implies. Now, very few Christians teachers have suggested that all 613 precepts of the Old Testament law should be observed by Christians.

In the first place, there's clear New Testament evidence that the Jewish apostles felt free to disregard the food laws, for example. Likewise, the whole of Paul's letter to the Galatians is an argument to convince non-Jewish believers that they don't need to follow the Jewish law or be circumcised in order to become Christians.

So usually people are selective about which parts of the law still apply to Christians, and how that might work. Perhaps it is only the Ten Commandments that still matter. Or perhaps what we might call the "ceremonial" laws are no longer relevant, while the "moral" and "civil" ones are.

The trouble with that way of thinking is that it is not so easy to divide the Old Testament law into distinct categories. Is the Sabbath law a moral or a ceremonial law? Isn't the whole law in some way about worshipping the one true God through right behaviour?

And some readers of the Bible have suggested that the Old Testament law has no ongoing relevance for the Christian life—other than perhaps the way Jesus summed it up as love of God and love of our neighbour (Mark 12 v 29-31). The fear is that the New Testament's emphasis on grace will be undermined by any suggestion that there are still things that Christians are *commanded* to do. It is so easy for us to slip back into trying to earn God's favour by doing things to impress him, the kind of legalism from which grace freed us in the first place.

The biblical frame around the law

I think there is an important biblical frame around this issue that helps us see a clear way through it.

First, we have to remember that the word "law", or *Torah*, refers not simply to the *commands* of the Old Testament but to *the whole of the first five books of Scripture* from Genesis to Deuteronomy. This means that the commands are not without a context: they were received in the middle of the liberation and redemption of Israel from Egypt and their entry into the promised land. In other words, **you can't read the laws without the story**—which is, of course, a story of the grace of God. The grace of God *precedes* the giving of the law, and not the other way around. It never was the case (as you sometimes hear people say) that in the Old Testament people were accepted by God through works, but now in the New Testament, we are accepted by grace. It was always by grace! But grace produces godliness, then as now.

Secondly, the laws themselves were never simply timeless moral truths for life anywhere at any time, but were a complex symbolic system for teaching Israel about the utter holiness of God and the need to be right with him.

To live under the law was to know the character of the God of Israel. And not simply to know his character: it was to be called to worship him rightly, as he directed. That's why the Ten Commandments begin with commands to worship God and only him. Sadly, these are the ones people often forget.

But thirdly, the law also **pointed forward** to its own need to be fulfilled or completed. People had to offer sacrifices for the forgiveness of their sins again and again, showing that the law itself was not sufficient to save. This makes sense of Jesus' teaching about the law.

Jesus preached against legalism—relying on law-keeping to be saved. Those who thought they had some grounds for ethnic and moral pride on account of the law were those he scolded the most. But the law itself was something he prized. The law is the script that Jesus himself lived out. It is his story in the end. He understood the inner purpose of the law—that it is about love of God and of neighbour—and he accomplished its purposes, by bringing people into relationship with God.

So, is the Old Testament law for Christian living? The New Testament authors do make quite positive use of the law as a guide for the Christian life in some places. In James 2, for example, the author uses the Ten Commandments as the standard for his discussion of holiness. Paul repeats Jesus' teaching about love as the central component and summary of the law in Romans 13. But it is not as if in doing so he says that anything in the Ten Commandments would be contrary to Christian life.

And this is perhaps key. The New Testament is saying that we are at a different point in the story. Holiness for the people of God looks different now because we are living in a new age, after the fulfilment of the law in the death of Jesus. But that doesn't make the law simply irrelevant. Is it Christian to worship God exclusively and rightly? Of course. Is it now right to kill, or to commit adultery, where once it was not? Of course not.

Love is a summary of the law, but love is not thereby simply exchanged for the commandments. The commandments, which are acted out in the life of Jesus, paint for us the colours of love.

Chapter 6

Is grace a licence to sin?

Does the fact that we don't earn our salvation by doing things to impress God mean that there's a free pass on sin? Can we, in Augustine's famous phrase, "Love God and do what we like"?

A powerful answer to this question can be found in the writings of Dietrich Bonhoeffer, which have spoken powerfully to subsequent generations of readers. One of Bonhoeffer's earliest books was his commentary on the Sermon on the Mount, entitled *The Cost of Discipleship*. It is a moving experience to read this book, knowing what would soon happen to the author himself. His reflections on "taking up one's cross" and "dying to the self" bite all the more deeply. We've already heard his challenging words: "When Christ calls a man, he bids him come and die". No one would live this out more than Bonhoeffer himself.

Bonhoeffer begins his book on Christian discipleship with a chapter entitled "Costly Grace". Costly grace is to be understood in part by contrasting it with what he called "cheap grace". But what can this mean, since God's grace is supposed to be free?

In the German Protestant church of his day, Bonhoeffer could see plenty of evidence of the cheap variety of grace, but not much of the costly sort. The Protestant church was founded on the teaching of God's free grace to us in Jesus Christ. But in Bonhoeffer's eyes, many thought that they could receive God's grace without needing to change in any way. Life could go on as if nothing had happened.

Bonhoeffer puts it this way:

> Cheap grace is the preaching of forgiveness without requiring repentance ... Cheap grace is grace without discipleship, grace without the cross, grace without Jesus Christ, living and incarnate.

Grace is not cheap because it is free; but, because it is free, by some it is held to be cheap.

No short cuts

The cheap grace of Bonhoeffer's experience is unfortunately alive and well in our own time. The "Christianity" of cheap grace is remorselessly nice. It is as bland as an easy-listening radio station. It is concerned with social approval and belonging, and risks nothing. It has misunderstood what Christianity really is. "Cheap-grace Christianity" also keeps theology at arm's length, as if it has nothing of any impact to say about the real world but is only a mental game we play.

What of costly grace? This may seem like a contradiction in terms. But Bonhoeffer reminds us of Jesus' parable of the treasure hidden in a field: the man who discovers it happily pays everything he can to possess it (Matthew 13 v 44). This grace is not simply a lucky prize that we didn't even buy a ticket for. It involves a call to follow Jesus to the cross.

It is perhaps not surprising that we find this teaching very hard to take since the first disciples found it difficult too. How could the coming kingdom of God really mean that they might have to follow Jesus even to his death? Was there not a short cut that did not involve this path?

There is no short cut. Grace costs nothing, but it demands everything. Bonhoeffer says:

> Costly grace confronts us as a gracious call to follow Jesus, it comes as a word of forgiveness to the broken spirit and the contrite heart. Grace is costly because it compels a man to submit to the yoke of Christ and follow him.

And that call doesn't come to just a select few—to a spiritual elite who can dedicate themselves solely to prayer and contemplation. That, for many centuries, was the church's response to the difficulty of this teaching. The heavy burden of discipleship was borne by the spiritual specialists: the monks and nuns, with their daily routines of prayer, and their disciplines of self-denial. But the challenge that Martin Luther, a former monk, gave to the church was to see that the call of Christ had come to every man and woman and not just some. Our discipleship cannot be outsourced.

That meant that discipleship had to be lived out in the world—not just by monks, but by farmers and bankers, by princes and the poor, and by parents with their children. There was no area of life to which the call of the gospel did not come, no territory exempt from the lordship of Christ. Luther learned from his study of the Bible that...

> the following of Christ is not the achievement or merit of a select few, but the divine command to all Christians without distinction.

But by Bonhoeffer's day, many so-called Christians had fallen for the lie that the grace of God offered in the gospel to the whole world automatically bestowed on humanity the blessing of God. The great doctrine of justification—by which sinners can be declared "not guilty" of their sin because of Christ's death—was taken to mean that because God had shown mercy to the world, his judgment against sin had been removed.

Was there any compelling reason for German Christians in the 1930s to reflect that something had gone badly awry within their culture? Apparently not, since they thought they could do as they wanted because of the grace of God.

Costly grace

But a grace which is presumed upon becomes something other than grace. It is a perversion of Luther's teaching; and (worse) a perversion of the teaching of the Jesus and the rest of the Bible. Grace, costly grace, comforts us in our sinfulness, but does not say "okay" to our sin. Costly grace is what shatters our faith in the world, and calls us to leave behind our old way of living.

For Bonhoeffer, the call of Christ meant standing against Hitler. It meant the loss of his academic career, his security, his chance to escape the grasp of the Nazis, his future marriage, his freedom and eventually his life. He would not have thought that this was extraordinary; but only rather what the grace of God in Christ had called him to do.

What would you say to a Christian who continues to sin?

First, I would say "stop!"

But we know all Christians continue to sin. That's part of living life this side of the new heaven and the new earth. We shouldn't deny that we sin, as 1 John 1 v 8-9 makes clear. That would be deceiving ourselves. Nevertheless, a sign that we have really taken hold of the grace that comes from God is our desire to remove sin from our lives and to live in a way worthy of the calling we have received.

A Christian who continues in a consistent pattern of sin needs to hear the gospel of grace again and again. The key to helping them change is the realisation that they have forgiveness and mercy. We need to see into the character of God himself. The cause of many of our sins is a failure to realise just how holy God is, on the one hand, and just how expansive God's love and mercy are, on the other.

The place where we see this is at the cross of Jesus Christ. By going to the cross of Christ, we realise that God's hatred of our sin is far greater than we thought; but his determination to overcome it in love is even greater. The more we know this, the more we will be motivated to see how petty and stupid our sins are.

The Bible gives lots of advice about how we are to rebuke, encourage and restore ourselves and each other, and plenty of case-studies of "failed followers" as both warning and encouragement to us. See Psalm 51; 1 Samuel 11 – 12; Galatians 6 v 1-2; James 4 v 7-10.

Chapter 7

How does grace change me?

> For the grace of God has appeared that offers salvation to all people. It teaches us to say "No" to ungodliness and worldly passions, and to live self-controlled, upright and godly lives in this present age, while we wait for the blessed hope—the appearing of the glory of our great God and Saviour, Jesus Christ, who gave himself for us to redeem us from all wickedness and to purify for himself a people that are his very own, eager to do what is good. *Titus 2 v 11-14*

The human will is a very mysterious thing. We know this, because we spend so much money and effort trying to change it. We try to trick it, to persuade it, to force it and to control it.

But the really odd thing about the human will is the way in which it forces us to have a dialogue with ourselves.

Ever tried to change a deeply ingrained habit? What keeps a smoker smoking, or an over-eater over-eating, even when they understand the horrible effects of their habit and know they want to change? Have you ever had that conversation with yourself where you told yourself you weren't going to lose your temper, but you did anyway? Or where you promised yourself you wouldn't tell another defensive half-truth, but you did anyhow?

Our world is full of advice on this subject. The self-help industry is keen to sell you its "secrets" for success. So, what are the solutions? Here are some typical responses:

- *Try harder.*
- *Follow the rules.*
- *Go to counselling.*
- *Take control of your life.*
- *Unleash the giant within.*
- *Believe in yourself.*
- *Man up.*
- *Get a grip.*

But do you notice the fatal flaw in these remedies? They ask us to be strong where we are weak. How can I believe in myself when I am so broken, without a colossal act of self-denial? How can I take control of something that is controlling me?

A new strategy for change

Paul says something entirely different about this vexed issue in his letter to Titus. What is his strategy for change? Shockingly, there is no strategy at all, other than *to know the grace of God*—which is not mysterious at all. There's no need to search; God has made it known. It is out in the open.

Let's think through how this works. By the grace of God—his kindness to us in Jesus Christ—comes an offer of salvation to all people, despite the fact that all people have been alienated from God in the darkness and shame of their sin. That's the bottom line. Even the enmity of human beings to the one true God is not an obstacle to the great offer of salvation by God's grace. In fact, that's what makes it grace: it is *despite* what we are, rather than *because* of what we are, that God rescues us by the blood of his Son.

And this very grace is the source of the kind of life a Christian then seeks to live. Apart from God's grace, there is nothing else we need to do this. So the gospel of grace is always needed throughout the Christian life. That's why Paul says that grace not only *is* our salvation but also *"teaches us to say 'No' to ungodliness and worldly passions"* (Titus 2 v 12).

It is not simply that we begin by grace: we go on by grace as well.

Teaching us about sin

The grace of God teaches us in the first place that God hates our wallowing in sin. His grace does not overlook sin, but tells us that sin is a very bad thing indeed—we needed rescuing!

Grace does not say to us: *You know, you are really OK deep down.* Grace does not teach us that our self-indulgence and our enslavement to our desires are actually nothing to worry about. God in his kindness—and it is kindness—tells us the truth about ourselves. We are exposed by the searchlight of his holiness—thank goodness. Because it's honesty that we need.

If God did not reveal to us the depths of our disgrace, then he would be showing us no kindness—like a doctor who tells a cancer patient that he has a bout of flu from which he will soon recover. Giving us the bad news *is* grace, because it makes it impossible to deceive ourselves any longer.

Overcoming sin

But the grace of God also teaches us that the power of sin to condemn us is now broken. We no longer face the wreckage of our lives unable to do anything about it. We no longer carry the oppressive weight of our past failures, which we can do nothing to change. We now no longer face the prospect of God's condemnation of us.

We find in the grace of God a tremendous freedom from the things that once enslaved us, from which we were powerless to free ourselves. We experience God's kindness to us, in that he suffered in himself the consequences of our personal failures.

And this is where grace is our teacher: it tells us not that we can be victorious over sin if only we try hard enough, but that God has already been triumphant over sin. The power of sin has already been broken at the cross of Christ. And knowing that is what teaches us to say "No", and to get a grip on ourselves.

The miracle is that this actually works at both a psychological and practical level. The genius of recovery programmes like Alcoholics Anonymous is that they trade on a kind of replica of the gospel of grace. They teach that you can't change without realising that you can't change by yourself. And they ask you to commit to utter dependence on a higher power.

I find it fascinating that even this shadow of the gospel actually really works to change people. How much more then, having heard and understood the real message of mercy and forgiveness, having grasped the depths of the true God's love for us in Christ, can we be free from the shackles of our passions and move forward into the life that God has designed for us to live?

How utterly humanising is the gospel of grace which comes and declares to us the blessing of our heavenly Father upon us! How extraordinary that by the kindness of God—by grace—we are given back ourselves and freed from the terrible battle with the enemy we call the self!

So, what now?

Here are some practical suggestions on how to make grace a reality in our lives. We will need to take action because we get so deeply stuck in the rut of ungrace.

1. **Deliberately practise giving thanks to God—for everything**. Actually setting aside time to be thankful reminds you that you are dependent on God giving you things, and especially for giving you Jesus.

2. **Practise doing good things that you don't have to do, as opposed to those things you are duty-bound to do**. God's grace is a model of extra kindness above and beyond. It is not necessary, but it is

abundant. Can you find opportunities to be generous and kind to excess?

3. **If you are stuck in a pattern of sin and are saying
to yourself: "I can't help it", then catch yourself.**
Your focus is on the wrong thing. Actually, you are
right: you can't help it—*on your own*. The verse in
Titus tells us that it is *always* possible to say "No"
if your mind is set on God's grace to you in Christ.
And that means...

4. **You need to keep going to church and to your Bi-
ble-study group.** Even if you feel rotten to the core,
you will be reminded once more of the grace of God
to you in Jesus Christ, as the Bible is opened and
read and explained, and as other Christians talk
with you about the great things he has done. Many
Christians who are struggling with sin stop attend-
ing church out of guilt and shame—and that's the
worst thing they can do. It means you are sadly left
trying to combat sin on your own, denying yourself
the help that God has provided when you need it
most.

And this last point is crucial. Grace isn't just something
that God works through our own lives as individuals.
It's something that shapes our communal life as believers too. In the next chapter we'll explore how...

Chapter 8

How does grace change us?

Not far from where I live in Sydney, in a park called Centennial Park, is a sandstone domed structure of no particular splendour. In fact, it resembles nothing so much as a public urinal.

Yet this building marks the spot where the constitution of the Commonwealth of Australia was signed on 1st January 1901 and the various colonies of the Australian continent became a nation. It's typical of Australia that one of its most significant historical sites is virtually unknown to its citizens!

A constitution is a document that gives an identity to a group of people. It expresses their agreed values and their vision for life together. It is a document that they can go back to in a crisis when they need guidance. In Australian history this has been tested in particular by the question of who should be included in the Australian ideal. It took six and a half decades before indigenous peoples were recognised as citizens, for example; and it wasn't until 1973 that an immigration policy that favoured "white" people was finally dismantled.

Who is in and who is out?

If there is one theme throughout the New Testament, it is the matter of who is "in" and who is "out" of the people of God. The Old Testament was the story of God's chosen people, the people of Israel—a nation of slaves called out of Egypt and made the objects of God's special favour. They were a racial group (with some exceptions), related by blood. They were the children of Abraham. This nation received God's promises of his blessing and his protection; and they were given the land of Canaan in which to live. This was their "constitution", if you like. Inclusion in this people was (it seemed) by being a descendant of Abraham, and was expressed in keeping the laws of the Old Testament.

However, there were hints in the pages of the Old Testament that this wasn't the full story. There were non-Israelites who were allowed to become Israelites, like Rahab the prostitute, and Ruth, the Moabite woman who became an ancestor of King David. The prophets likewise continually reminded the people that taking for granted your membership of the people of God meant risking that very membership.

Now fast-forward to the New Testament. The extraordinary thing about the Christian message is that it includes non-Israelites—which was plainly shocking to almost everybody. How could this be possible?

It makes sense because, as the New Testament fully

reveals, the constitution of the people of God is not blood and race, but the grace of God, received by faith.

Feeling legitimate

This is what drives the marvellous words of the letter Paul wrote to the Ephesians, a group of Gentile believers living in what is now Turkey. How could the good news about a Jewish Messiah be good news for them? What claim did they have for membership in the people of God?

> For it is by grace you have been saved, through faith—and this is not from yourselves, it is the gift of God—not by works, so that no one can boast. For we are God's handiwork, created in Christ Jesus to do good works, which God prepared in advance for us to do. Therefore, remember that formerly you who are Gentiles by birth and called "uncircumcised" by those who call themselves "the circumcision" (which is done in the body by human hands)—remember that at that time you were separate from Christ, excluded from citizenship in Israel and foreigners to the covenants of the promise, without hope and without God in the world. But now in Christ Jesus you who once were far away have been brought near by the blood of Christ.   *Ephesians 2 v 8-13*

You have to remember for a moment what it feels like to not be included. We all know that feeling at some level: whether it was a moment in the school playground, or an invitation to a wedding that never came, or a time when our opinions were simply ignored because we were the wrong gender or skin colour.

That is the feeling that Paul is seeking to overcome: the feeling of illegitimacy. And how does he reassure his Gentile readers? He reminds them that God chose them from before the foundation of the world, choosing them "for adoption to sonship through Jesus Christ …to the praise of his glorious grace, which he has freely given us in the One he loves" (Ephesians 1 v 5-6).

This is grace. They are members of the people of God because his people are brought together by the grace God gives freely in Jesus Christ. All have sinned, Israelite and Gentile alike. All need the grace of God—and in the death of Jesus, the two are made into one new people. He is our peace.

And we can't ignore the profound implications of this truth. Here are some:

1. **If the people of God are brought together by grace, and not by race or ethnicity or culture, then there are absolutely no grounds for any racial or ethnic division in the Christian church.** It is simply a denial of our constitution! This should make us think very carefully about how we express our national identity in the Christian meeting. It also should make us concerned when only one kind of people are coming to our church, especially when the local community is very different. Are only beautiful/educated/European people at your church? Is everybody about the same age? Then is

there a condition for membership in your community other than grace? *Could be...*

2. **If, in fact, belonging to the people of God is by grace, and not by works or by ethnicity or privilege, then we should treat others with the same grace that has been shown to us.** That's very often the message of Jesus' parables—not simply that God saves us by grace, but that, as those saved by grace, we ought to treat others with the kind of patience and forgiveness that we have been shown. Grace is in our DNA as the church of God in both membership and our relationships. We don't belong on any other basis than the grace of God in the death of Jesus. So we don't exclude others because of skin colour or ethnicity. But neither do we look down on, or exclude from our friendships within church those who mess up, are social misfits, have criminal records, get themselves into debt, or have complex, chaotic families.

3. **We must never, ever be boastful of who we are and what we've done—except to boast of the grace of Christ.** One of Paul's great themes is humility. "Where, then, is boasting?" he asks in Romans 3 v 27, in the middle of explaining how the gospel includes both Israelite and Gentile. The answer is: *Boasting has no place!* There is no achievement involved in belonging to the people of God. Quite the reverse. You cannot be proud of it, for all it says of you is that you are a sinner who has accepted a free gift. So you cannot act with anything but humility towards others.

This then is the constitution of the people of God: it is grace. It is by the grace of God that his people are gathered together, and by no other thing.

The gifts

And God equips his people for their life together by giving them gifts. In Ephesians 4 v 7, Paul writes:

> But to each one of us grace has been given as Christ apportioned it.

He then goes on to explain that Christ gave the various roles in the church to make sure the church was bonded together in unity. It is just the same language that he uses in Ephesians 3 v 7-8 to talk about his own calling to be an apostle in—as a grace given to him for the sake of the gospel.

The same kind of thought is behind the most famous passage on spiritual gifts, 1 Corinthians 12 – 14. There Paul talks about the spiritual "gifts" or "graces". They are given to members of the church. It's the purpose of the gifts that matter. What makes them truly spiritual is that they achieve the purpose of God's Holy Spirit, which is to build up the church. In this way they are a continuation of the grace by which God gathered the church in the first place.

So what do you do with your gifts? The way some Christians talk about spiritual gifts, you'd think they were at a self-help seminar! The thing to ask is not: *How can I express myself with my gifts?* but: *How can I serve God's people?* Use your gifts not to lift yourself up, but to build up the people of God. Spiritual gifts are not about self-expression.

That actually might mean *not* using them at times. There may be several gifted preachers at one service, but only one preacher is usually invited to preach. For the most part, you don't have every drummer in the congregation drumming at the same time. So you may need to hold back, if that's what serves the congregation best. Likewise, cultivate and practise your spiritual gift in order to make yourself a better servant of God's people. Get a certificate in administration or accountancy, perhaps; or take some music lessons; or learn how to operate the sound system properly. If building others up is the goal, then that should be your motivation.

Am I unforgiven until I ask for it?

I once had a Christian friend who asked me: "What if I tell a lie to my parents, then walk out of the house and get knocked over by a car. Am I forgiven for that sin? I haven't confessed it or repented." It's an important question that troubles many Christians in one way or another.

The Bible encourages us not to deny we are sinners, but to confess our sins as part of our ongoing Christian life (1 John 1 v 8-9). And many Christian churches have the practice of saying a prayer of confession as part of their meetings. Unfortunately, this can sound as if we have to keep "squaring accounts" with God or else we risk losing our salvation.

But the Bible is equally clear that our salvation is given to us as a one-off, all-inclusive deal. The New Testament speaks as if *all our sin*—past, present and future—has already been forgiven (Ephesians 4 v 32; Colossians 3 v 13; 1 John 2 v 12). The Holy Spirit comes to us as we receive the gospel and secures our salvation. We do not need to keep making a new sacrifice for sins every week; we already have the one sacrifice for sins for all time.

It is a good thing for us to confess our sins and be reminded of the forgiveness we have in Jesus so that we will learn not to sin, and so that we will be clear in our conscience. But that doesn't mean that you have put your salvation in jeopardy by not recalling some sin you committed eight years ago, which, because you haven't asked specifically for it to be forgiven, is still held as outstanding business.

The answer to my friend's question was first: "Don't sin!" But second: "Be assured that if you are in Christ you are a new creation" (2 Corinthians 5 v 17). Even if you die with an unconfessed sin, you will be fully and completely forgiven and accepted.

Chapter 9

How bad are human beings really?

ow bad are human beings? It would have to be admitted that the obvious answer is "pretty bad".

Just to take one very modern example, there seems to be no end to the stories in the media about the bad treatment of people on Twitter. Anonymity is a veil from behind which it is apparently ok to unleash torrents of abuse at people, even when a person is well known for their struggle with depression.

Expecting better

But anyone who is a parent or teacher knows that a key tactic in helping children to behave is to expect better of them. Somehow, they will rise to meet the standard expected of them.

Aren't human beings as a whole like this? If we say: *It's no good: they're simply evil and always will be,* won't we get what we expect? Doesn't it make sense to say to people: *Not only is doing good something you ought to do; it is also something you can do?*

This very modern debate is actually as old as time itself; It was fiercely contested among Christians some 1,600 years ago.

Pelagius was a monk and theologian from the British Isles who took morality—and the moral responsibility of human beings—very seriously. He lived through a time in which a great civilisation, the Roman Empire, was decaying around him. He would have been witness to tremendous and brutal evils in his time, living as he did around the sack of Rome in the early fifth century.

His teaching was not that human beings are naturally good—that doctrine would have had no credibility at all among those who had seen limbs hacked off and heard the screams of rape victims. Rather, he held that men and women were free to choose the right or the wrong. Each of us could, should and would be held fully accountable for our actions. He argued that we ought to hear the full impact of God's address to his people: "Be holy, because I am holy" (Leviticus 11 v 44), or Jesus' words: "Be perfect, therefore, as your Father is perfect" (Matthew 5 v 48).

For Pelagius, this meant what it says. Surely Jesus would not have said it if it was not a moral possibility. He would not have given us a task we could not accomplish, difficult though it may be. Moral pessimism is insulting to the Creator of human beings, who made not puppets or beasts, but people. It is a view that he was able to back up with powerful arguments.

Is the first step ours?

This is how Pelagius described it: Think about what happens when you do anything. There are three aspects to it. There's your *ability*, or power, to do the act; your *intention* to do it; and the actual moment when you put your power and your intention together and realise the *action*. As Pelagius thought of it, the ability that we have to act comes from God. But our intentions and the realisation of our actions belong to us. In other words, when we choose to do the right thing, we can count on power from God to aid us. But it is we who choose it. The first step is ours.

It isn't too hard to see what made, and still makes, Pelagianism attractive. First, like most convincing heresies, it could appeal to biblical sources. The commands of the law and of Jesus were surely commands that could be carried out and ought to be taken seriously.

Secondly, it was the remarkable lives of holiness that Christians had lived in the first years of Christianity that had been perhaps the most remarkable testimony to the truth of their cause. Pelagianism was a call to return to this source of strength in the face of social chaos.

Thirdly, Pelagianism is a theology that seems to treat us like individuals and like adults. It demands that we put aside childish excuses, and take responsibility each for our own actions. It requires of us discipline and hard work; it calls us to virtue.

Fourthly, it is positive about humankind in a way that seems to honour the Creator's stamp on us. Human beings have a high destiny indeed serving so majestic a God and seeking to imitate him.

We cannot actually do it

But the Pelagian movement ran headlong into arguably one of the stoutest defenders of biblical orthodoxy the church has ever seen: Augustine of Hippo, theologian of grace.

His first reply to the Pelagian teaching was to agree with this at least: human beings as made by the Creator are glorious creatures, possessing a true freedom—the freedom not to sin, being endowed with a good will and an inclination to do the right thing.

However, this is where Augustine disagreed: *Adam fell.* The fault was entirely with him; there was no way in which God could be blamed for his lapse. His will, free to not sin, had the possibility of choosing wrongly. This first sin didn't just affect Adam, because in that sin a greater fall occurred than in any of the myriad sins that followed it. Here, Augustine was thinking of Romans 5 v 12:

> Therefore, just as sin entered the world through one man, and death through sin, and in this way death came to all people, because all sinned...

The result of Adam's sin, Augustine argued, is that human nature is terribly scarred and deformed. In every aspect, human beings are now enslaved to sin and destined for death. We are ignorant, lustful and dying. We have lost, above all, the use of that free will not to sin that Adam enjoyed. We cannot now avoid sin; sin hangs around even our "good" deeds, as a bad smell over a corpse. We may still have a free will, but now we only use it to choose wrong.

The killer blow against Pelagianism is the very fact of human behaviour, throughout history and across cultures. We, who live in the wake of the horrors of the terrible 20th century, ought to know this more than anyone in history. As critic George Steiner once said:

> We know that a man can read Goethe or Rilke in the evening, that he can play Bach and Schubert, and go to his day's work at Auschwitz in the morning.

Pelagius' teaching, and those who think like him in modern times, fails simply on account of the fact that human beings, even when they *know* what the right thing is, *cannot actually do it.*

But if the effects of sin loom large in Augustine's teaching, it is because the power of grace is overwhelming. His pessimism about human nature leads him to conclude that Pelagius must be a deceiver, encouraging in men and women pride in thinking they can free themselves from the mire. Without God's help we cannot, says Augustine, overcome the temptations of this life.

And God's help—his grace—cannot be merely a matter of external aids, such as the teaching of Jesus about the godly life. Augustine was able to see that Pelagius had a shrunken view of the cross as God's free gift. And more than that a defective view of the Holy Spirit. He sees him not as the free gift of God giving himself to us and giving us a whole new birth, but as a moral kick in the rear, or just a great example.

If we were once dead in our sins, then how are we now alive to God in Jesus Christ by his Holy Spirit, and truly freed for doing the works of God? Surely it can only be by the mercy and grace of God!

Although Pelagianism as a movement was discredited by Augustine's arguments back then, it remains very much alive and well; and it takes both secular and religious forms. You see it in the moral tales of cartoons aimed at children. You detect it in the journey of heros in popular movies who make a choice between good and evil. You hear it from politicians. You read it in novels. And you hear it preached from far too many pulpits. Partly this is because the need for moral teaching and guidance has never been more pressing. But in large measure it is because it appeals to our pride to believe that we have the power to change ourselves.

On the other hand, we have forms of deterministic ideas about our thinking and behaviour that need repudiating. We are being told that our choices and morality are determined by our genes, for example, or that society is to blame, or our parents. It amounts to a moral cop-out.

It may be tempting to want to believe and pass on these modern versions of Pelagianism in the teeth of that kind of moral laziness. But we need to remember that what you and I need more than anything is not better ethical training. What we need is the powerful gospel of forgiveness and new life. In other words, the gospel of sheer, beautiful, free grace.

Other titles in this series

Why did Jesus have to die?
by Marcus Nodder

Our culture ignores it. Many within the church seem to be almost embarrassed by it. Many others understand that the cross of Christ is at the very heart of Christian faith and life. This short, readable book explains clearly and simply what the Bible, and Jesus himself, says about the cross, and how Christians should understand it today.

Is God anti-Gay?
by Sam Allberry

Christians, the church and the Bible seem to be out of step with modern attitudes towards homosexuality.

In this short, simple book, Sam Allberry wants to help confused Christians understand what God has said about these questions in the scriptures, and offers a positive and liberating way forward through the debate.

See the full range at your local Good Book website:
UK & Europe: www.thegoodbook.co.uk
North America: www.thegoodbook.com
Australia: www.thegoodbook.com.au
New Zealand: www.thegoodbook.co.nz

thegoodbook
COMPANY

Opening up the Bible

At The Good Book Company, we are dedicated to helping Christians and local churches grow. We believe that God's growth process always starts with hearing clearly what he has said to us through his timeless word—the Bible.

Ever since we opened our doors in 1991, we have been striving to produce resources that honour God in the way the Bible is used. We have grown to become an international provider of user-friendly resources to the Christian community, with believers of all backgrounds and denominations using our Bible studies, books, evangelistic resources, DVD-based courses and training events.

We want to equip ordinary Christians to live for Christ day by day, and churches to grow in their knowledge of God, their love for one another, and the effectiveness of their outreach.

Call us for a discussion of your needs or visit one of our local websites for more information on the resources and services we provide.

UK & Europe: www.thegoodbook.co.uk
North America: www.thegoodbook.com
Australia: www.thegoodbook.com.au
New Zealand: www.thegoodbook.co.nz

UK & Europe: 0333 123 0880
North America: 866 244 2165
Australia: (02) 6100 4211
New Zealand: (+64) 3 343 1990